Surviving the

IDITAROD

AN INTERACTIVE EXTREME SPORTS ADVENTURE

by Nicki Jacobsmeyer

CAPSTONE PRESS
a capstone imprint

You Choose Books are published by Capstone Press,
1710 Roe Crest Drive, North Mankato, Minnesota 56003
www.mycapstone.com

Library of Congress Cataloging-in-Publication Data is on file with the Library of
Congress and available at the Library of Congress website.

ISBN: 978-1-5157-7170-8 (library binding)
ISBN: 978-1-5157-7174-6 (eBook PDF)

Editorial Credits

Nate LeBoutillier, editor; Bobbie Nuytten, designer; Eric Gohl, media researcher;
Katy LaVigne, production specialist

Photo Credits

Dreamstime: Rvestal, 61; iStockphoto: cweimer4, 17, 79; Newscom: Jeff Schultz, 6, 74,
94, Reuters/Nathaniel Wilder, 10, SIPA/BONY, 26, 32, 51, ZUMA Press/Adn/Loren
Holmes, 1, 4, 41, 44, 56, 65, 70, 83, 89, 102, ZUMA Press/Bill Roth, 107, ZUMA Press/
Bob Hallinen, 22; Shutterstock: dramaj, back cover, Josef Pittner, 47, Matt Cooper,
cover, Michael Roeder, 106 (bottom), Sergey Uryadnikov, 106 (top)

Printed and bound in Canada.
010382F17

TABLE OF CONTENTS

ABOUT YOUR ADVENTURE

YOU love sled dogs and the thrill of the trail and have always dreamed of running the Iditarod. Your dream is about to come true.

The Iditarod is one of the world's boldest competitions. It is a race by dog sled that covers approximately 1,000 miles and cuts through the heart of the Alaskan wilds. It takes mushers anywhere from about a week to two weeks to complete — if they can actually finish the course.

The choices you make will guide the story and determine the outcome. Will you cross the finish line in glory? Will you fail in the cold and snow? You choose.

Turn the page to begin your adventure.

CHAPTER 1

LEADER OF THE PACK

It's late February and the snow is perfect for dog sledding in Alaska.

You've worked especially hard throughout the past year running, resting, and camping with your dogs. You pride yourself on building a strong dog team. You've practiced running your dogs along various glacier trails to prepare for icy terrains.

You've circuit-trained to build up your own endurance, strength, and flexibility. With a few local mid-distance races under your belt and having recently celebrated your 18th birthday, you're now fully qualified to run the Iditarod.

Turn the page.

You've grown up working in your family's kennel. It boards Alaskan Malamutes, Alaskan Huskies, Siberian Huskies, and mixed breeds. These dogs are all bred for the trail and perform best in freezing temperatures.

You ran the Copper Basin 300 race using Quint, your big silver-coated Alaskan Malamute, as lead dog. If you showed frustration with Quint, he wouldn't perform. However, his endurance and stamina made him an excellent leader in the windy, subzero temperatures.

Your team finished strong in another 300-mile race with Arrow, your Alaskan Husky, as lead. Arrow's long-haired toe pads provided traction on the frigid river. The white-coated mixed-breed with visible strains of Samoyed *did* have a tendency to wander. But when Arrow focused, she led the team efficiently.

Tanner, your dark-coated Siberian Husky with sharply-defined face markings, ran lead as you competed in the Junior Iditarod. Tanner's speed beat the average pace of 8 to 10 miles an hour. There were times he showed his stubbornness, but when your eyes met his — one blue and one brown — he knew not to disobey. In the end his speed and agility were invaluable.

Each of the qualifying races gave you an opportunity to see how your lead dogs performed in different circumstances. As a musher you never know what you will encounter along the trail. Which dog has what it takes to lead your team across the arctic tundra of the Iditarod?

To race Quint as your lead dog, turn to page 11.
To race Arrow as your lead dog, turn to page 45.
To race Tanner as your lead dog, turn to page 75.

The Iditarod's starting point is located in Anchorage, Alaska.

CHAPTER 2

STRENGTH OF THE PACK

It's the first Saturday in March. Iditarod fans line Fourth Avenue in downtown Anchorage, Alaska. Competitors have come from all over the world to test their teams' strength over 1,000 miles in the Alaska wilderness. These men and women, 18 to 70 years old, all have their eyes on the finish line in Nome. The races consist of 50 to 70 teams all eager to start down the trail.

You check the dogs and gangline for the tenth time.

"How are you feeling?" asks a Swedish musher parked next to you.

Turn the page.

Your nerves have stolen your voice.

The musher straps on his red fur hat. "Good luck," he says, grinning. "Enjoy the Last Frontier!"

You're instructed to line up in the starting chute where a new team starts every two minutes.

"Alright Quint, you ready?" you say to your leader. "It's our first Iditarod, buddy!"

Quint barks in excitement.

This is it. The time has come to see if you're ready for this. Your heart beats like thunder. Sweat moistens your palms. Your gut churns.

"Three . . . two . . . one . . . " shouts the announcer. "GO!"

The dogs bolt out of the chute. Your ears fill with the hearty cheers of your family, friends, and well-wishers.

As the announcer says your name over the loudspeaker, you're overcome with emotion. After a few blocks, you make a hard right turn. The trail runs through sparse woods and tunnels beneath the streets.

In the tunnel's darkness, your sled shimmies and jerks. You exit the underpass and look down to see your team colliding into each other.

Quint is trampled and whines when his leg gives out. The team scrambles to get up and into position. Quint continues on, but he's favoring his back right leg.

The unfamiliar tunnels have unnerved your dogs. You haven't even reached the first checkpoint, and you're already worried about your lead dog.

To keep Quint racing, turn the page.
To rest Quint in the sled bag, turn to page 20.

Quint is vital to your team, and he's a fighter. You push on with him in the lead. You arrive at the town of Willow, the official start of the race. You're thankful when the Iditarod veterinarian there finds minimal swelling on Quint's leg.

Another 180 miles down the trail, you find yourself struggling with extreme fatigue. Maneuvering through the Happy River Steps and Dalzell Gorge has you aching all over.

The fallen snow swirls in the air making visibility awful. Your eyes strain to see down the line. You praise the team one by one. "Looking good, Quint," you shout. "You're my strong boy, aren't you?"

You count your dogs and then blink to refocus. You left Rainy Pass with sixteen dogs. Did you just count only fifteen?

You wonder if your eyes are playing tricks on you. You stop the dogs, lay down the snow hook, and begin to count, touching the head of each dog as you do so. ". . . thirteen, fourteen, fifteen. Foster? Where's Foster?"

You count again, carefully. Foster's gone.

You must check in with the same number of dogs you checked out with at the previous checkpoint. You have to go back.

To head back to the checkpoint, turn the page.
To stop and rest your team first, turn to page 19.

You need to find Foster. How in the world did he get loose? Did you forget to clip him to the gangline?

"Haw! Haw!" you shout, instructing the dogs to go left and turn around.

Quint looks at you in confusion but obeys. The final checkpoint of the day is more than three hours away. This mistake is going to cost you.

The dogs' gait is sluggish. Maybe they can make one last push before resting.

"What do you say, Quint?" you holler to your lead dog.

To keep the current pace, go on to next page.
To increase their speed, turn to page 32.

You've pushed your team to its limit. A slower pace will have to do.

Another team approaches. "Easy," you tell your dogs. "Easy now."

The Iditarod trail is a challenge for even the most experienced dog-sledding teams and mushers.

Turn the page.

Feeling foolish that you're going the wrong way, you explain. "I lost a dog," you shout to the passing musher. "Did you see one at the checkpoint?"

"Black and white?" the musher shouts, slowing his own team.

"Yeah," you say. "With a scar by his eye."

"Saw a lone black and white dog, but I don't know about a scar," says the musher. "Was poking around near the crooked tree."

Relief spreads through you. "Thanks!" you shout. You take a deep breath and focus on your destination.

Turn to page 34.

Your dogs will suffer if you don't give them a break. They stagger off the trail.

You don't have any straw to bed down the dogs. You survey the wooded surroundings. The spruce needles lying on the snow make good insulation. You set about assembling makeshift beds. You feed your dogs a cold, stale meal from your emergency food in the sled.

You inspect the gangline where Foster was stationed. It's been gnawed through. When did that happen?

You're too weary to think about it anymore. All you need is a few minutes to rest your eyes, and then you'll be able to solve the mystery.

Turn to page 34.

Quint needs time to heal. The official start isn't until tomorrow in the town of Willow. The teams will take off one-by-one and the race clock will start.

Your decision to rest Quint pays off. He looks strong out of Willow. Just after noon on Day 3 your team leaves Rohn, 188 miles out.

You pass Farewell Lake and drop in to the barren Farewell Burn. In 1978 this was the site of Alaska's largest forest fire. You steer your team through fallen trees, dirt, and rocks. The visibility is crystal clear as you run from ridge to ridge.

There's not a soul in sight. Your fatigue is extreme so you tie yourself to the sled. When you inevitably doze off on these 90 miles of desolate country, you won't be left stranded.

You nod off and awaken to the shouting of a filthy, hunched-over man shuffling down the trail toward you.

"Stop!" the man cries as you bring your team to a halt. "You're going the wrong way!" His beady eyes dart back and forth.

"Go that way," he says pointing east. He shambles off in that direction.

You rub your eyes to refocus. When you open them, the man is gone.

Are you going the wrong way? Or has your exhausted imagination run wild?

To ignore the man's warning, turn the page.
To listen to the man's warning, turn to page 24.

You must be hallucinating. A common occurrence in the Burn.

"Hike!" you shout.

Quint's nose is to the trail. His instinct is true and you're rewarded for trusting it when you arrive in Nikolai a couple of hours later.

You give your dogs a frozen salmon snack as they rest. You're mentally drained and need to get off your feet. You sprawl out by your dogs.

"Hey, there," says a veteran musher. "How you holding up?"

"Barely," you mumble.

"You've made it through the toughest part," says the musher. "Your 24-hour rest is right around the corner."

You smile weakly. "Right around the corner," you reassure yourself.

Turn to page 30.

You can't believe you're going the wrong way!

"Gee!" you order.

Quint hesitates.

"C'mon boy! Gee," you bark.

Quint's ears go down as he leads the team east.

After half an hour you start second-guessing yourself. The trail hasn't been broken. You stop the team.

You hear someone call your name. You snap your head toward Quint to confirm. He's busy licking his paw. You realize that you're losing your mind. The village man is a hallucination. Now you're lost in the Alaskan Interior!

You head on back the way you came, feeling discouraged.

Finally, you get your team back on the trail. You find a fellow musher and follow him on in to Nikolai.

You'd love to take a long, quality break in Takotna, where there is less activity and noise. The checkpoint in Takotna, however, is 66 long miles away. Taking a rest in McGrath, 48 miles away, might be more realistic. It's not as peaceful as Takotna, but it's closer.

To rest in Takotna, turn the page.
To rest in McGrath, turn to page 30.

You're sticking to the plan and not stopping. You push through the checkpoints with minimal rest. It is a race, after all.

On the sixth day you make the run to Takotna during the warmest part of the day. The sun beats down.

Some of your dogs have diarrhea, Quint included. The 40-degree temperature is a heat wave in these parts. Your team struggles into Takotna.

"Your team isn't looking so good," says the veterinarian, frowning.

"They're dehydrated," you reply.

As the vet gives the dogs medicine, you set to work getting them food and water. You know they need more than the daily gallon of water in this unexpected warm weather. You spend more time than planned at this checkpoint caring for your dogs.

Turn the page.

It's Day 9 of the Iditarod. The Bering Sea coast awaits. Temperatures plunge below zero with a windchill factor of nearly 100 degrees below Fahrenheit.

"Weather report just in," the staff member announces in the Kaltag community center. The mushers perk up. "A storm is hitting the coast. Low visibility and snow. You're advised to stay here until it clears."

Storms are common on the coast and can be challenging. You're probably stuck. But then you remember a story you read. According to the story, sometimes mushers camp out in the vacant cabins along the coast if the weather gets dangerous.

You spot Michael, a rookie from Wasilla, across the room.

Michael shakes his head and says, "Can you believe this storm?"

"I'm wondering how bad it really is," you say.

"Hard to say," Michael says. "I did hear there are cabins on the coast."

"I heard that too," you reply.

Michael smiles. "You must be bold and brave to run the Iditarod."

"Yeah," you say. "Or nuts."

To stay in Kaltag, turn to page 36.
To head for the Bering Sea coast, turn to page 38.

You turn the corner eight hours later.

"Welcome to McGrath!" The checker looks at her clipboard. "Are you declaring your mandatory 24-hour break?"

"Yes, we're staying," you say, as your team is guided to an open area.

A man with kind brown eyes stands nearby, observing the teams. Soon the dog team is devouring hot beef stew with kibble and then falling asleep. You head toward the building.

"Strong team you have," the man says, catching you by surprise.

"Yes, sir. Thank you," you reply.

"My name is Nutaaq, a native Inuk of this land," he responds.

"Hello, Nutaaq," you say.

Nutaaq smiles and says, "You should be warned that not everyone is supportive of this race."

"Can we talk later?" you ask. "I've got to get some sleep."

Nutaaq smiles and nods as you walk away.

You don't know what to make of Nutaaq's comments, so you put them out of your mind. You head inside and use the coin-operated shower. Then you head to the kitchen and gobble down steak, eggs, and apple pie.

You're so tired after eating, you can't keep your eyes open. You settle in to sleep hard and fast. After 24 hours, you're all recharged and ready to blow out of the checkpoint. You jump on the sled when you see Nutaaq. He waves to you.

To stop and talk to Nutaaq, turn to page 40.
To wave to Nutaaq and race on, turn to page 42.

You have to find Foster. Your mind starts racing. What if he's lost? What if a wild animal has confronted him? What if he's hurt?

"Hike!" you screech to the dogs.

You see another team coming your way.

"Have you seen a lost dog?" you ask as your teams pass.

"Nope, sorry," the musher replies, continuing on the trail.

Without thinking twice, you sprint your dogs down the trail. Finally, you make it to the Rainy Pass checkpoint.

"My dog," you say to the checkpoint volunteer before your sled has even stopped, "have you seen my dog? He's black and white with a scar by his eye."

No one has seen Foster.

A call goes out over the radio to begin a search. You can't go on until all your dogs are accounted for. Hours go by without a word. A day passes, and then another.

You're beaten. You're heartsick. You lost your chance of finishing the Iditarod. Worst of all, you lost a dear friend.

THE END

To follow another path, turn to page 9.
To learn more about the Iditarod, turn to page 103.

You pull into the Rainy Pass checkpoint for the second time. Thankfully, Foster is there, curled up under the tree. You throw down your snow hook and go to him. He barks and wags his tail.

"We figured you would be back," the smiling vet says.

"Is he okay?" you ask.

"Yes," the vet replies. "He sure was missing his team and two-legged friend."

"We're all here, boy," you say.

Foster licks your face in forgiveness.

Now that you've stopped moving, you don't know if you can get back up. Your legs feel like tree trunks rooted to the ground. You look at your furry family. Their eyes plead for a break.

You find their paws raw. Too many of your dogs are beat up to continue racing. It's time to go home.

You lie down next to Quint and enjoy his warmth. He has been a devoted lead dog.

Your experiences on the trail have taught you many lessons. You know with this knowledge and more training, your team will be back to try again next year.

THE END

To follow another path, turn to page 9.
To learn more about the Iditarod, turn to page 103.

You look around the room. No one else is packing up. "I'm going to stay," you decide.

"Agreed," says Michael.

You go out to check on your dogs. They are so full of energy that you consider changing your mind. But you know better.

News comes in that two mushers are missing. They both left Kaltag before the weather advisory, more than 20 hours ago. The Iditarod Air Force searches, but there's no sign of anyone.

Everyone is silent after the news. Each musher knows the gamble when racing in a storm.

Finally, the next day, the storm comes to an end. As you mush down the Bering Sea coast your mind keeps recalling the missing mushers. You worry they won't be found or you too will get lost in the Arctic abyss.

You pull into the checkpoint called Safety, some 22 miles from the finish line. You learn that the two missing mushers showed up later in Unalakleet.

When you reach Nome, you no longer have to fake your happiness. Your team made it across the Alaskan outback. Together you ran "The Last Great Race on Earth."

THE END

To follow another path, turn to page 9.
To learn more about the Iditarod, turn to page 103.

"I'm going. I want to finish in the top half," you say.

"Be careful," says Michael.

You set out and the headwind slaps you across the face. You crouch down on your sled to make it easier for the dogs. Quint leads with determination.

You pass Tripod Flats and Old Woman Cabin and decide not to stop.

You reach the open tundra. The snowdrifts make it impossible to see ahead. By the feel of it, you're barely moving at all. It's time for you to lead your team. You pull the gangline with all your strength but make little progress. The wind uproots you from the ground.

A mighty gust of wind flips your sled onto its side. The storm pushes you to the ground as you crawl. You reach your sled and pull the dogs toward you. The sled blocks the wind and you share body heat.

You hope someone will pass by soon. But deep down you know you're fooling yourself. No one is coming out in this storm. Not unless they're a fool like you.

The shivering subsides, and you grow hot. You attempt to take off your parka, but you're too exhausted. Your eyes flutter. Finally, you decide a short nap will do some good. You close your eyes for the last time.

THE END

To follow another path, turn to page 9.
To learn more about the Iditarod, turn to page 103.

You know talking to Nutaaq will take valuable time, but you feel it's necessary. A vital part of running the Iditarod is to honor Alaskan culture.

You put out your hand. "Thank you for your devotion to the land, Nutaaq."

He smiles and says, "Those who truly honor this land and its animals shall prosper."

He seems to have nothing more to say, so you simply shake his hand and race into the night.

The dogs come alive in the cold. A sparkle catches your eye. A vivid display of northern lights illuminates above. You watch the colors dance across the sky. The swirling movements seem to guide you.

As you press on you feel a connection with your dogs and the land. You wonder what challenges and adventures await you.

Iditarod mushers are occasionally treated to some of nature's finest sights, such as the Aurora Borealis, or Northern Lights.

With Quint as your lead dog, your team is ready for whatever comes your way.

You're a rookie whose dream was to be an Iditarod musher. And now you are. Together you finish the race in Nome, happy and fulfilled.

THE END

To follow another path, turn to page 9.
To learn more about the Iditarod, turn to page 103.

You'd like to talk to Nutaaq, but you need to run. You wave and hope he's not upset with you.

It seems your hurry is paying off when you soon catch another team out on the trail. The musher gives you the right of way, and Quint charges past. As you contemplate how much farther till Takotna, your headlamp sputters out. Darkness smothers you and your team. You take a deep breath and relinquish the trail to the dogs.

"Alright, Quint," you say. "It's all you, friend."

You hear a distant rumble that puzzles you. There are only shadows. The back of your neck tingles. A bright light shines as a snowmobile plows out of nowhere through the clearing toward you.

You have no time to react. "NO!" you scream.

The rider on the snowmobile doesn't brake, crashing through your sled and your team.

You're thrown into the air. When you crash-land, pain shoots up your arm. You look around. The snowmobile sputters away, its driver dressed all in black. You have no idea what just happened. It was so fast.

You search for Quint as you struggle to get to your feet. Quint is unscathed. Some of your dogs are injured, but none life-threateningly.

Tears roll down your cheeks. Quint licks your face. *Why?* you wonder. You wonder if Nutaaq was trying to warn you of such a thing.

You can't believe someone would sabotage a dog-sledding team. You wonder who it was and why they did it. The reckless disrespect of one person nearly killed you and your dogs and destroyed your chance to finish the Iditarod.

THE END

To follow another path, turn to page 9.
To learn more about the Iditarod, turn to page 103.

CHAPTER 3

EAGER TO RACE

The second day of the Iditarod brings relief. Your team can survive a night in the Alaskan wilderness. You mount the sled and whistle as your team barks, as usual.

The sun shines off Arrow's white coat. You reach for your sunglasses. Arrow's dark and almond-shaped eyes are protection enough for her.

The team curves around a patch of trees as you put on music for the remaining 40 miles to Finger Lake. Arrow and a few of the dogs hesitate.

"What's wrong, girl?" you ask Arrow as you reach the clearing. Arrow and the dogs halt.

Standing in the middle of the trail is a moose crowned with enormous antlers.

No one moves. The 500-pound animal could inflict major damage with one swipe of his hoof or antlers.

The dogs bark, alerting the moose. His ears lie back. What are you going to do? The fate of your team lies in your hands.

To wait till the moose leaves, go on to the next page.
To go around the moose, turn to page 50.

Your team is a safe 50 feet away but then they start another round of howls.

"Quiet."

The moose will wander off if it doesn't feel threatened. The dogs fidget.

Your eyes dart to the moose. He shows the startling whites of his eyes and smacks his lips.

Turn the page.

The moose charges. Arrow leads the team off the trail. It's not enough time.

The moose's massive front hooves smack Spade in the head and wipe out two more dogs.

After that, the moose traipses off into the woods. You carry the wounded in your sled bag to Finger Lake. The sled bag holds your supplies and has room for a few dogs.

When you enter the Dalzell Gorge you're cold and weary. The moose attack and dropping three dogs have made you anxious.

Thankfully, Arrow looks sharp through the glare ice and open water of the Dalzell Creek.

The trail thins at the bridge. You're going much too fast!

"Easy, Arrow!" you shout.

The team creeps over the bridge when your sled slides toward the edge. You lose your footing and grab hold of the sled bag. The team drags the sled as you dangle above the sloping ice.

"Hike! Hike!" you plead.

As they cross to the other side, you lose your grip. You slide into the piercing water.

Your clothes are drenched. You're at least an hour away from the warm sanctuary of the Rohn checkpoint.

To change your clothes now, turn to page 59.
To wait and change later, turn to page 62.

"Gee," you instruct the team to go right, off the trail.

The moose follows your movements with his coal-colored eyes. Arrow keeps quiet, silently instructing the other dogs. Soon the moose becomes a distant spot. You breathe a sigh of relief and move on.

Some of the worst trail in the race lines the path from Rohn to Nikolai, so you follow another team out. The trail is nothing but dirt, rock, sand, and driftwood.

"As long as we see Egyptian Mountain drift behind us on the right, we're on target," David, an experienced musher, says.

"Sounds good," you reply.

A few miles through the woods you glance over your right shoulder. Where's the mountain?

"David?" you shout.

"Yeah?" he replies as he looks behind him.

He scans left and right.

"Whoa!" he stops his team.

David's face says it all. You've lost the trail.

Turn the page

Your teams arrive in Nikolai 18 hours later.

"Arrow, how's my girl?" you say, examining her paws. They're red and swollen.

Out of habit, you turn to your drop bags for supplies and come up empty.

An Iditarod Committee member approaches you. "I'm sorry but I have bad news. Your drop bags didn't make it to Nikolai," he says.

"What do you mean?"

"They were left in Anchorage by mistake."

You're baffled by the news. You needed that drop bag. Your sled bag, as is, has minimal food and supplies, which you could spread thin to hold you over till McGrath. But you and your team could sure use a rest — though that would sap supplies.

To set out immediately for McGrath go on to the next page.
To rest in Nikolai, turn to page 55.

You've arranged for 64 bags spread down the trail. Not one made it to Nikolai. You feel you have no choice but to go to the next checkpoint.

The other dogs move sluggishly when Shiloh and Melody start coughing. Your spirits drop.

As you swing northwest, the town of McGrath appears. With a brave final push, Arrow looks like a wounded soldier pulling the team in.

The dogs collapse in your designated resting spot. When you locate your drop bags you almost weep with joy. The triumphant moment is ripped away by the vet's news.

"Unfortunately, Shiloh and Melody have pneumonia," the vet says. "Their race ends here."

Your shoulders sag. You go to pet Shiloh but become distracted.

Turn the page.

Arrow is leaving a trail of red drops. You crouch and examine her front paws. They're bleeding. Her booties have thinned to almost nothing.

"Oh, Arrow," you whisper.

As the vet checks them over you begin to make the dogs' stew of beef, chicken fat, and guts.

The vet approaches you. "The dogs need rest. I would advise you to take your 24-hour break now," the vet says.

Maybe you should quit before your entire team breaks down.

To quit and scratch the race now, turn to page 64.
To wait and decide till your break is over, turn to page 65.

You will have to make it work. The team needs to get off its feet. You save the protein for the dogs. You eat a few cubes of butter for energy.

It's Day 10 and the Bering Sea coast is howling your name. The temperature is minus 55 degrees. The wind whips at 40 miles an hour and starts a ground blizzard, swirling the already fallen snow all around you. Your dogs push on, determined to get to Shaktoolik. You squint through your snow goggles and see that Arrow has lost her booties.

"Whoa!" you shout repeatedly.

You go to Arrow and try to put on a fresh pair of booties with your thick mittens.

When you remove them to work quicker, the wind sucks the warmth out of your fingers. They go numb. You pull the mittens on with your teeth, only able to cover half your hands.

Turn the page.

Soon you pull into the main street of Shaktoolik. Inside, you determine most of your fingers are white, but some have black patches.

You look up at the checkpoint volunteer, Pamela. She frowns and says, "Let's get you some help."

You're staring at your hands when you hear Arrow howl.

To patch up your hands, go on to the next page.

To check on your team, turn to page 67.

Frozen fingers can lead to frostbite in the cold climate of Alaska.

"Let's get you taken care of first. You're no good to them if you can't use your hands," Pamela says.

"Will it take long?" you ask.

"It may take several hours for a doctor to get here," she says.

"I can't wait that long. Will there be a doctor at the next checkpoint?"

"Later in Elim," she confirms.

"We'll go there," you say.

She wraps your hands with sterile gauze and puts on your mittens. You thank her and get moving.

When the team arrives in Elim, Arrow's bark wakes you from dozing off, which happens from time to time to mushers.

Turn the page.

Your eyelashes are frozen splinters. Your mind is working in slow motion.

The doctor says you could lose a finger or two if you continue. But you're less than 100 miles from Nome. You have the doc rewrap your hands, and you enjoy several bowls of moose stew, the bowl warming your hands as you slurp from it.

Arrow's loyalty keeps the other dogs happy as you travel down the coast to White Mountain. The pain in your fingers is soon forgotten when your stomach begins to cramp. Your forehead dampens and beads with sweat.

As you instruct the dogs to go faster, the nausea and bloating hit you. You don't know why, exactly. When you pull in at the White Mountain City Hall, you're going to need to throw up.

To run inside and take care of yourself, turn to page 69.
To stay outside and take care of your dogs, turn to page 72.

Wet clothes in these frigid temperatures can be deadly.

You walk over to the birch trees and remove a few strips of bark. You collect dry twigs and cardboard from your sled bag. You strike a match and the birch bark ignites quickly.

You change clothes, and the dogs nap while you force your eyes open. After an hour you get antsy. Your skin is no longer chalky white.

Arrow expertly leads you through the Rohn checkpoint and the Alaskan Interior with no problems. You realize that you have luckily escaped hypothermia.

Your Alaskan Husky's efficiency is paying off. Out of Ophir there are only two teams ahead of you.

Turn the page.

Whoever makes it first to the halfway mark at Cripple walks away with a trophy and $3,000 in gold nuggets, a nod to Alaska's flashy gold-mining industry.

After a seven-hour run, you rest for a few hours on the Innoko River. Later, you see one of your competitors camped out in the open river valley.

"Hike, Arrow!" you shout.

The team feeds on your energy and opens up its stride.

You don't pass anyone before you pull into Cripple but you're pleased with the dogs' efforts.

"Welcome to Cripple! Congratulations!" the check-in volunteer says.

You look at him, surprised.

Sled dogs go through a good number of booties on the Iditarod trail.

"You're the first musher to arrive," he replies.

You can't believe your good fortune. As you stand with the sponsor holding $3,000 in gold nuggets you're certain you and your team will make it to Nome.

THE END

To follow another path, turn to page 9.
To learn more about the Iditarod, turn to page 103.

You don't want to lose momentum now by stopping. You mount the sled with shaky limbs. Back on the trail, your body shivers and your cough gets worse.

You struggle through chores in Rohn with a pounding headache. The vet finishes checking the dogs and gives a good bill of health.

"You aren't looking so good, though," the vet says.

"Not feeling too good," you say.

"Let's get you medical attention," the vet says.

Soon it's determined you have stomach flu and mild hypothermia. You drift off but feel worse when you wake hours later.

An Iditarod official approaches you and asks, "How you feeling?"

"Awful," you say, cocooned in the blankets. "How many more miles to Nome?"

"About eight hundred," he replies.

You rub your head. Even thinking is painful. You can't sit up at the moment, let alone race a dog team.

"I'm too sick to go on," you whisper. "I'm done."

Not stopping to take care of yourself was a mistake. Your fear of losing an hour has cost you the race. The thought of taking Arrow and the team home without finishing pains you. You roll over and bury your head under the covers.

THE END

To follow another path, turn to page 9.
To learn more about the Iditarod, turn to page 103.

You can't believe you let it get to this point. You know better. A team must finish with a minimum of five dogs. If this pattern keeps up you might not even have that many.

Your attitude stinks. You're at rock bottom. This isn't fair to your dogs. Right now you're leading them into disaster. You aren't even halfway done.

You plop down by your team. You've failed. You hang your head and sigh as Arrow licks your face.

THE END

To follow another path, turn to page 9.
To learn more about the Iditarod, turn to page 103.

You feel mentally and physically plowed over. You need to rest before deciding to scratch.

You spend the next day caring for your team. It's just what you all needed. Arrow's paws have healed nicely and she's in better spirits.

Luckily, you and the vet decide, only two other dogs need to stay behind. The well-being of your dogs is more important to you than any race.

Rest is important for sled dogs after a hard day of racing.

Turn the page.

The same thought crosses your mind on Day 12 when you and 11 of your dogs make it to Front Street in Nome. Your dogs are family. They're the reason you're crossing the finish line.

The crowd cheers as you hug and praise each dog for its hard work. You're no longer a rookie and have plenty of tales to tell. You proudly wear your Iditarod finisher's belt buckle now that you are officially a part of the club.

THE END

To follow another path, turn to page 9.
To learn more about the Iditarod, turn to page 103.

"Let me see to my dogs first," you say.

You tend to your team as quickly as possible and head back inside.

"The doctor is on his way from Elim," Pamela says.

You curl up in a corner and get some sleep while you wait.

Later, an older man shakes your shoulder and your eyes fly open.

"Sorry to wake you. I'm the doctor. I need to take a look at your hands," he says.

He asks questions and examines your hands.

"You have severe frostbite. We need to thaw your hands in warm water immediately," the doctor says.

Turn the page.

"Which means?" you ask.

"You would have to scratch. You can't expose your hands to these temperatures anymore," he responds.

"What if I keep going?" you ask.

"You'll most likely lose fingers," he answers.

You struggle with his response. You don't want to let down your team by scratching. If you lose fingers, your ability to care for the dogs will suffer. Then there may not be another race in the future.

With a heavy heart, you scratch. Not finishing the Iditarod is a disappointment. However, not being able to take care of your dogs the way they deserve is unthinkable. You, Arrow, and the team will be back next year with all hands on deck.

THE END

To follow another path, turn to page 9.
To learn more about the Iditarod, turn to page 103.

After throwing up for 20 minutes straight in the hall you can hardly stand up.

Jordan, an Iditarod committee member, enters the room, searching for you.

"I'm coming," you say. "I think I've got food poisoning." You race to the bathroom.

Jordan knocks. "What can I do?"

You hold your head in your hands. The room spins. "Can you bed the team down?" you ask.

"You know what happens if I do, right?" Jordan asks.

In your disorientation you'd momentarily forgotten about that rule: No outside help allowed.

"Ugh," you say. "I can't let my dogs suffer."

Jordan says, "So what's it going to be?"

Turn the page.

You take a deep breath as you process the inevitable. "I scratch," you say. "Please, please go take care of my team."

"Don't worry," Jordan says. "I'll take care of your dogs."

You're not sure if it's a wave of sadness or nausea, but you get sick again.

Mushers are constantly looking out for their dogs at checkpoint stops.

The next thing you remember is hearing a loud engine. You're on a stretcher and Arrow is barking. You look around in alarm.

"It's alright," Jordan says, "You're on a helicopter with your dogs on the way to Nome. You need to go to the hospital. You're very sick, but you and your team are going to be alright."

You start to wonder where it all went wrong. The guilt and remorse try to pull you down. Right when you think you might give in, Arrow licks your hand.

Jordan is right. As long as you are with your dogs, everything will be alright.

THE END

To follow another path, turn to page 9.
To learn more about the Iditarod, turn to page 103.

You run to the side of the City Hall and vomit. The stench burns your nostrils. You work through stomach cramps and vomiting in shifts. Your hands get rewrapped for a temporary fix.

You leave White Mountain much later than the mandatory eight hours you must stay to rest. At this point just finishing the race will be a win.

You hear the sirens when you hit Front Street in Nome. You can hardly keep it together. Your arms clutch the handlebars. You haven't eaten in hours because nothing stays down. You're exhausted, lethargic, and in pain.

However, crossing that finish line is one of the happiest moments of your life!

You collapse off the sled. People rush toward you with helping hands. Arrow and the other dogs take turns licking your face as you praise them.

Before the festivities come to an end, you're awarded the Most Inspirational Musher Award for this year's Iditarod. The award is chosen by fellow mushers. They vote for the musher whose positive attitude motivated them to continue down the trail. You can hardly wait to tell your family and friends.

THE END

To follow another path, turn to page 9.
To learn more about the Iditarod, turn to page 103.

CHAPTER 4

NEED FOR SPEED

Heading out of the Finger Lake checkpoint, 123 miles down the trail, you focus on the Alaskan Range. It's the most difficult part of the race.

The first challenge is the Happy River Steps that climb up and down a canyon. You take the advice of veteran racers to run this leg when the sun is up.

"Hike!" you shout, to encourage your team.

Your lead dog, Tanner, doesn't even pause when he reaches the top. You catch your breath as your team disappears over the valley. They race down the curved trail without slowing.

Turn the page.

"Easy, Tanner!" you yell.

The icy trail becomes switchbacks sending you down the canyon step by step.

Trees line the trail. Any wrong move will mean a broken bone or worse. You slam down on the sled's brake. It doesn't slow the momentum of your dogs.

The last step plunges your team onto the frozen Happy River.

"Whoa! Whoa!" you scream as you propel off the sled with only one hand clenching the handlebar.

Your team isn't stopping. You could be beaten to pieces if you hold on. If you let go you will be left behind in the vast wilderness.

To let go of the handlebar, go on to the next page.
To hold on to the handlebar, turn to page 86.

You relinquish your hold on the handlebar and your huskies run out of sight. You scramble to your feet and take off running.

Soon, another team approaches.

"Lose your team?" a burly musher with a beard asks.

"Yes," you reply.

"Hop on. We have a team to catch," the musher instructs.

You jump on his sled bag. As you come around a bend, your huskies are at a standstill. Your sled is caught in a rut that has prevented them from running.

"I can't thank you enough," you say.

"No problem. It's happened to me many times," he says as his team moves on.

Turn the page.

The Alaskan Interior is brutal. You leave the town of Cripple and pass the site of Poorman. In 1911 this gold mining ghost town was in its prime.

You head to the Ruby checkpoint, the beginning of the Yukon River. You inhale the fresh, crisp air of the Alaskan wilderness. As you exhale, a round of coughing begins. You reach for a drink of water, hoping it will help.

No such luck.

Your chest tightens. You begin to wheeze. You know that your asthma is acting up. You reach for your inhaler in your sled bag. You try to stay calm as the frosty air seeps into your lungs.

You shake the inhaler and press down. Nothing comes out. You try again.

Nothing.

Your inhaler has frozen when you need it most. Worse yet, the Ruby checkpoint is still 8 miles away.

To race to Ruby for help, turn the page.
To stop and regroup, turn to page 81.

Without your inhaler, you're in serious trouble.

You need to slow your breathing down and open up your lungs. You balance yourself on the sled. You put your hands over your head to open up your lungs. Thankfully, you find some relief.

The village doctor in Ruby is a welcome sight. You're immediately given the proper medicine that stops the asthma attack.

"You will need to rest here for a day or more," the doctor says. "The delay in medication and the freezing temperatures inflamed your lungs."

You follow the doctor's orders. The next day, you're rewarded with permission to leave.

Turn to page 83.

You pull off the trail and stop. You may not make it to Ruby alive if you keep going.

Luckily, when preparing for the race, you researched what to do if you were separated from your asthma medication. But reading about it and actually dealing with it are two different things.

You start a fire and place your inhaler nearby to defrost it. While you take care of the dogs you drink from your thermos. The villagers at the last checkpoint were kind enough to fill it with hot coffee. The warmth relaxes your airways.

You take shallow breaths as you struggle with your one-person tent. You climb inside and focus on breathing through your nose. You crawl into the insulated sleeping bag.

Turn the page.

When the wheezing slows down, you risk moving and seeing if the inhaler has thawed. You can hardly believe it when medicine puffs out of the inhaler. You take the proper dose and relax as the medicine does its job. Soon you're feeling better and on your way to Ruby.

You don't stay long at the Ruby checkpoint. You take care of the dogs' needs and close your eyes for a few minutes. An hour later you get up and notice a crowd of mushers. You wipe the sleep from your eyes and go outside.

A blanket of snow covers your team. You look toward the checkout area and can't see the trail. Reports indicate the storm will continue through the night. Do you want to be the first to break trail?

To let someone else break trail, go on to the next page.
To break trail with your team, turn to page 85.

Breaking new trail saps even the best dog teams' energy. Trudging through mounds of untouched snow packs each dog's paws and underside with snow and ice.

After letting a couple other teams leave first to break trail, your team functions well. The lashing wind blows the snow into your dogs' faces the entire stretch to Kaltag. The dogs push through with determination. They almost look happy to be in this weather. But for how long?

To stop in Kaltag, turn the page.
To continue down the coast, turn to page 90.

Resting in the village of Kaltag gives you time to restore your energy before you reach the coast.

Kaltag has a water pump that will save time instead of melting the snow. It also has real toilets instead of portables.

The dogs enjoy their stew and straw beds. They're always priority one. You grab food from your drop bags and chow down on candy bars and jerky. The villagers are always welcoming mushers at the checkpoints with hot, homemade treats as well.

The snow hasn't let up and is covering the trail marks. No one seems in a hurry to leave.

One more stretch remains down the Bering Sea coast. If you wait, the storm could worsen. You get the team ready to leave before you change your mind.

You're hoping that Tanner is ready to use his endurance and maneuvering skills.

Tanner gets the team down the trail but not without a fight against the hurricane-force winds. Your surroundings are bleak, nothing but snow and frozen sea.

Tanner begins to strain on the gangline. Shakespeare and Everett, the swing dogs behind Tanner, aren't pulling their weight. They both stop as though they've hit a wall. The team pauses in confusion.

"Hike!" you shout through the whipping snow.

Your swing dogs have stalled.

You know some dogs get scared of the white stretch of landscape on the coast and won't budge.

To change the dogs' positions, turn to page 91.
To keep them in their current positions, turn to page 93.

The advice of veterans repeats in your head. "Never let go of the handlebar."

The dogs drag you down the trail. Rocks jab your chest while your legs ricochet off the trees. The team finally stops. Pain shoots through your body. You crawl up the sled.

Tanner takes you up the Happy River Hill and you head west through the forest. You distract yourself with the beauty of the Alaskan Range when you hear gunfire. The teams' ears stand straight up.

"Easy, Tanner," you say as you survey your surroundings. Up ahead you see a team stopped. A tall, lean musher is leaning over a large object.

"What happened here?" you ask.

"Moose," he answers. "It came out of nowhere and charged my team."

"Anyone hurt?" you ask as you approach his team.

"Thankfully, no. Spooked, I'm sure," the musher says.

"I'm still spooked myself," you say. "My team dragged me down the trail. There isn't a spot on me that isn't beat up."

"The Steps?" he asks.

"How'd you know?" you say.

The musher collects tools in his sled bag to gut the moose as required. You know any musher that passes by must help. But you're injured and don't know if you're physically capable of helping.

To help the musher gut the moose, turn the page.

To keep going because of your injuries, turn to page 95.

"Let me give you a hand," you offer.

"Thank you," the musher says.

You get to work but start having trouble keeping the bile down.

You head back to your sled bag and swipe a glob of vapor rub under your nose. The menthol will cover the smell of dead carcass. It also hides the smell when dogs are in heat, so that's why you keep it on hand.

Half an hour later the musher thanks you, and you head out.

You're ecstatic when you pull into Ruby several days later. Your dogs seem healthy and happy but tired. The grind from the Ophir and Cripple checkpoints has your team ready for an eight-hour layover.

Dog-sled teams mush on through the dark of night.

Once the dogs are resting with full bellies, you head toward the community center log cabin. A flash of yellow catches your eye. You see a man in a yellow parka kneeling by a dog team. He looks right and left. When you see the man give one of the dogs a shot, you at first assume he is a vet. He stands and turns your way with a guilty smile.

You're surprised to see that the man wears a racing bib number. He isn't a vet — he's a musher. And what he's doing looks very suspicious.

To turn the musher in, turn to page 97.
To keep what you saw to yourself, turn to page 98.

You're making good time and want to keep going. The wind and freezing temperatures take your breath away as you head out of Unalakleet.

You complete the second of the three Blueberry Hills. The head wind is unbelievable and you want to rest, but this is no place to camp. Tanner pulls the team to the top of the last hill. The snow swirls, making vision impossible. Time crawls. You look at your watch. It has been seven hours since you left Unalakleet. You should be in Shaktoolik by now.

You stop the dogs and look around. Nothing but a white canvas. You can't see any trail markers in the blizzard. You're lost on the Bering Sea coast.

You wonder how long you'll survive with what little supplies you have and the deadly weather.

THE END

To follow another path, turn to page 9.
To learn more about the Iditarod, turn to page 103.

If you want to stay ahead, you must take action.

Your oldest dogs, Sebastian and Granada, take the swing position. They have more experience running in the coastal weather than Shakespeare and Everett. With Tanner, they lead the team over the icy coast with no problems. Their confidence settles the dogs' nerves.

You make a brief stop in Safety. The finish line is only 22 miles away and you race for the lead.

You're ready to leave when one of your competitors yells, "Good luck!"

"Same to you," you smile, loving the adrenaline racing through your system.

When you pass Cape Nome you glance behind you. You can see another team barreling down the trail.

Turn the page.

You make it to the east end of Front Street and know the burled arch at the finish line is only half a mile away.

The flashing red and blue lights of your police escort don't spook the dogs. They seem to know what this means, and thrive on it.

You don't risk looking over your shoulder again. You hear a commotion behind you but refuse to take your eyes off the finish line.

"You got it, Tanner!" you shout.

The cheers ricochet off the buildings. Signs wave, and cameras flash.

You pull into the fenced-in chute for the last hundred feet. Tanner and the dogs race under the arch in triumph. You've just won the Iditarod!

THE END

To follow another path, turn to page 9.
To learn more about the Iditarod, turn to page 103.

Shakespeare and Everett need an extra boost of confidence.

You jump off the sled and hold the gangline as you head to the front next to Tanner. You lead the dogs down the icy trail.

You glance back and their tails are sagging. You give it another try.

"That's it, boys. Good job!" you encourage.

The dogs get in the zone and begin a steady pace. But the snow increases and the extra traction slows the dogs down.

You hear crackling. You glance down and water seeps up between cracks in the ice. Before you can yell to the dogs to hurry, Tanner takes off. The snapping of the ice paralyzes Shakespeare and Everett.

Turn the page.

Terrain of all sorts awaits sled
teams in the Alaskan wilds.

You search for a bank, drift wood, or
anything stable to get your team to. There isn't a
lifesaver in sight.

The ice divides under your team. The sea
begins to swallow you, one by one.

As you fight for your life, the Bering Sea
shows no mercy.

THE END

To follow another path, turn to page 9.
To learn more about the Iditarod, turn to page 103.

"I wish I could help," you say, "but I can hardly race."

"I understand," he responds.

"Good luck," you offer as you steer the dogs around the animal.

Soon, your team is on the stretch from Rainy Pass to Rohn.

You brace yourself for the next obstacle of the Dalzell Gorge. The trail gets narrow and windy through the trees. A "Watch Out" sign posted on the trail makes you cringe.

"Whoa!" you command.

The dogs stop as instructed, but your sled tips over the 200-foot hill.

"Oh, no!" you shout. "Hike!"

Turn the page.

The momentum of the sled barrels down the hill, taking your dogs along. The sled flips over. You hear the loud thud of dogs hitting the sled. The tumbling stops when you all smash into the canyon floor.

You wiggle your toes but can't feel your legs. The silence is not comforting.

You feel Tanner rub his wet nose on your hand. You strain in frustration as tears trickle down your cheeks. "Someone will help us, boys," you assure them. "You'll see." But you know no one will.

You look at Tanner for comfort as you lie paralyzed in the Dalzell Gorge thinking about the musher you let fend for himself.

THE END

To follow another path, turn to page 9.
To learn more about the Iditarod, turn to page 103.

You walk into the community center in disbelief. You've heard about some mushers using illegal steroids. You've got a feeling that's exactly what's going on here.

You scan the room for an Iditarod race judge. If the dog's musher won't protect his team, you will. You report what you saw with a heavy heart. The judge thanks you. The need to be with your dogs lures you outside. Soon you hear that the musher was disqualified. You're saddened to hear of that kind of disrespect for the sport.

You stretch out next to your dogs for a rest. When the time comes, you hit the trail again. Eventually, you cross under the arch in Nome. Well out of the top 10, you wear your finisher's belt buckle with pride. You ran a fair race.

THE END

To follow another path, turn to page 9.
To learn more about the Iditarod, turn to page 103.

The musher in the yellow parka stares at you. You stare back. You walk inside the community center. Surely, you misread the situation. You're caught off guard when one of the Iditarod race judges approaches your table.

"How is everyone holding up?" the judge asks.

Other mushers reply while you feel your body tense up.

"Enjoying your first time out?" he asks.

You see the musher with the yellow parka enter the room. "Yes, sir," you stutter.

The judge pats your shoulder before walking away. The musher gives you an angry look and storms back outside. You're too exhausted to deal with him. You go take a snooze. The alarm goes off and you shuffle out to your team. As you feed them again, the race judge approaches.

"We've had a report that you've injected one of your dogs with an illegal drug," the judge states.

"Me?" you ask.

"Yes. Do you deny these charges?" he asks.

"Yes, sir. I would never use illegal drugs," you answer.

"Can I see your veterinarian paperwork, please?" the judge asks.

You reach in your sled bag pocket. As you pull it out an empty syringe tumbles out.

"What is this?" the judge asks.

You stare at the needle, baffled.

"Sir, I promise you this isn't mine," you say.

The musher in the yellow parka catches your eye. He's smirking at you.

Turn the page.

Unbelievable. He set you up!

"I know what's going on here," you say.

"Please explain it to me," says the judge.

You tell the judge what you saw before you went into the cabin to rest. You believe the musher set you up to protect himself.

"I'm not proud of keeping quiet, sir, but I would never hurt my dogs," you say.

The judge folds his arms across his chest. "There's only one way to find out," he replies.

The chief veterinarian takes urine samples from both dog teams. The results conclude that your team is clean but the other musher is guilty of steroid use. The three-member judge panel determine he is disqualified from the race.

When you're finally allowed to continue, you've lost a lot of time. You have a long ride ahead to think about your actions. You spend much of it being disappointed in yourself for not turning the musher in. You weren't thinking about the health of the dogs or the sport.

When you arrive in Nome, it's bittersweet. Even though your team was clean, you finish the race far from contention and feeling guilty. Your first Iditarod adventure wasn't what you thought it would be. At least you've gained an experience — and hopefully some wisdom.

THE END

To follow another path, turn to page 9.
To learn more about the Iditarod, turn to page 103.

CHAPTER 5

THE LAST GREAT RACE

The Iditarod Trail Sled Dog Race is unlike any other competition in the world. With a team of sixteen dogs, each musher races 1,000 miles across some of the roughest and most desolate terrain in Alaska. Mushers must navigate their sleds over an obstacle course of mountains, frozen rivers, and desolate country through constantly changing weather.

The annual event takes place in early March and takes mushers from 8 to 15 days to complete. The race begins in Anchorage and ends in Nome. In even-numbered years the race takes the northern route, which consists of 26 checkpoints. In odd-numbered years the race consists of 27 checkpoints on the southern route.

The first Iditarod race was run in 1925 when a diphtheria epidemic threatened Nome, Alaska. The closest serum was in Anchorage, which was 1,000 miles away. Due to the sub-zero weather conditions, the only way to transport the 20-pound cylinder of serum was by train and dog sleds. On January 27, the serum arrived at the end of the rail line at Nenana. There, the first of 20 teams relayed the serum the final 674 miles to Nome. Five days later, on the morning of February 2, Gunnar Kaasen and his lead dog, Balto, arrived in Nome with the life-saving serum. This event went down in history as "The Great Race of Mercy."

The race was revived by Joe Redington, Sr. in 1973. Of the 34 teams that started the race that year, only 22 finished. Dick Wilmarth and lead dog, Hotfoot, finished in 20 days 49 minutes to take first place.

The first woman to finish the Iditarod was Mary Shields in 1974. In 1985 Libby Riddles became the first woman to win. Following her was Susan Butcher, who won three years in a row.

On average, some 70 mushers race across Alaska in the modern running of the Iditarod. Dog teams pull sleds weighing 150 to 200 pounds in gear alone. Sleds must contain an Arctic sleeping bag, snowshoes, an ax, a parka, a headlamp, batteries, dog booties, and two days of food for mushers and their dogs. Competitors may also carry medicine, changes of clothes, and a gun for protection from wild animals.

In 2017 Mitch Seavey and his lead dogs, Crisp and Pilot, set a new record for the fastest winning time: 8 days, 3 hours, 40 minutes, and 13 seconds. Seavey beat his son, Dallas Seavy, who had won four of the previous five Iditarods.

DANGERS of the Iditarod

Weather

Temperatures below zero, in addition to being uncomfortable, can be tough on equipment as well as on dogs and mushers. Blowing snow and the howling winds of blizzards can shut down progress altogether. And then there's weather that's too warm and causes melting snow and sloppy trails.

Wild Animals

Moose, caribou, buffalo, and wolves head up the list of animals that can be a danger to mushers and dog teams. For this reason, mushers carry guns with them to defend against attacks.

Fatigue

In addition to the threat of dehydration, ulcers, hypothermia, frostbite, snow blindness, and broken bones, extreme fatigue is a constant danger for mushers out on the Iditarod trail. The extreme lack of sleep and proper rest adds up over the 8 to 15 days it takes to complete the Iditarod course. Mushers who aren't at their physical best are more prone to making poor decisions.

GLOSSARY

asthma (AZ-muh)—a condition that is marked by difficulty in breathing with wheezing and chest tightness

checkpoint (CHEK-poynt)—a point or place where an inspection is carried out

dehydration (de-hy-DRAY-shuhn)—the loss water or body fluids

disorientation (dis-or-ee-uhn-TAY-shun)—the condition of being confused or lost

frostbite (FRAWST-byt)—the freezing of skin or deeper layer of tissues on some part of the body

gangline (GANG-lyn)—the main line that the dogs and sled are attached to

hypothermia (hy-po-THER-me-uh)—reaction of the body to an abnormally low body temperature

musher (MUSH-uhr)—person who travels over snow with a sled drawn by dogs

remorse (re-MORS)—deep regret for having done wrong

scratch (SKRACH)—to withdraw from competition

steroids (STAYR-oydz)—man-made hormones that are used in medicine to help tissue grow and increase muscle size and strength, which may have harmful effects and are usually considered illegal in sporting competition

traipse (TRAYPS)—to walk or wander about

unscathed (un-SKAYTHD)—completely unharmed

OTHER PATHS TO EXPLORE

◆ Two families, the Mackeys and the Seaveys, have developed Iditarod dynasties. Dick Mackey mushed in the first modern-day Iditarod in 1973 and won the event in 1977 by just one second — the closest finish in Iditarod history. Dick Mackey's son, Rick Mackey, won in 1983, and Lance Mackey, another son, won four times straight starting in 2007. Mitch Seavey, the son of Dan Seavey — who also mushed in the first modern-day Iditarod in 1973 — won in 2004, 2013, and 2017, setting the record for fastest finish and oldest victor at age 57. Mitch's son Dallas Seavey finished second to his father in 2017. In 2012 he became the youngest musher to win the Iditarod at the age of 25. He also won in 2014, 2015, and 2016.

◆ Many awards are bestowed to mushers in the Iditarod beyond crowning a champion. There are awards for best rookie, most improved, best sportsmanship, most inspirational, and best lead dog. In addition, the final finisher of each running of the Iditarod wins the Red Lantern Award for sticking to it and not giving up.

READ MORE

Hamilton, Sue. *Iditarod*. Minneapolis, Minnesota: ABDO Publishing, 2013.

Osborne, Mary Pope. *Dogsledding and Other Extreme Sports*. New York: Random House Books for Young Readers, 2016.

Paulsen, Gary. *Woodsong*. New York: Simon and Schuster, 2013.

INTERNET SITES

Use FactHound to find Internet sites related to this book.

Visit *www.facthound.com*
Just type in 9781515771708 and go.

INDEX